THE NEW ME IS BACK!

Dedicated to the two greatest loves of my life: MERRY and DORA

BASKET ONE:
Struggling with Writing

YOU GOTTA START...

You gotta start writing
no matter how bad...
The mind may be blank...
The soul may be sad...

Get to the paper
and put it all down...
Don't even worry
what might come around...

Just get to the writing -
Fill up the page
with thinking and nonsense...
with ranting and rage...

Cuz there on the paper
Your feelings will fall...
and most of the stuff
won't matter at all...

And most of the writing
will not do a thing...
But - you can be certain -
'something' will sing...

Something will matter...
So, get it all down...
It may be a verb...
It may be a noun...

But there in the rhyming
some pieces will fit...
and some of your longing
will settle a bit...

And some of your burden
will just disappear...
so, write, write and write...
and get your mind clear...

And go with the rhythm
wherever it leads...
The journey itself
Is one of your needs...

You gotta start writing...
So, take the first hop...
and, second of all -
You gotta not stop...

MAY 18, 1992

Five, eighteen and ninety two…
Time to start...to write...to do…
Time to stand...to walk...to run…
I have only just begun…

Nothing novel...nothing new…
I have started quite a few…
I begin and then I quit…
Never got the hang of it…

Good at 'starts' - but here's a clue:
Bad at things like 'follow-through'…
Bad at 'faith' and 'thinking-clear'…
(Guess I'll finish this next year…)

To Hell with the Title

I have refused to keep working my meters...
I will not bother to bother these lines...
Sitting here, thinking, repeating repeaters...
Nothing's as weary as overworked signs...

Thinking a thought and remolding its message...
Trying to clothe it in quality rags...
No ! I won't do it ! I'm done and I'm thru it...
Couldn't care less if it shows and it sags...

When I was younger I tortured my feelings...
Questioned each hope as it fell on the page...
Saddled my spirit with form and with structure...
Tightened the lid on my soul and my rage...

God only knows just how deeply it smoldered...
(He's not the type that keeps sifting the past.)
Whether it blew with a bang or a whimper -
Hey, I'm just grateful I lived thru the blast...

Now, I just think 'em, and then I just write 'em...
Letting them bounce to the place where they rest...
You - you can read 'em, forget 'em...or leave 'em...
If you remember just one - I am blest...

3 by 5 Card

I thought I'd try a pome upon a card…
and thought, at first, it might be kinda hard…
but see, at last, it's really rather nice…
The margins make the meters quite concise…

The bound'ries keep the sayings short and sweet…
and so, the rhyme and rhythm's very neat…

And tidy-minded people will agree:
it's very much more easier to see
the gist and meaning of the poet's mind…
(A funny lot - these tidy-minded kind.)

3 by 5 Card II

And when tomorrow comes around
With all its thunder...
And I awake to face
The hammer coming down,

I'll be O.K., my friend,
so don't you wonder...
For one more time I'll
pick myself up off the ground...

And I will take another step in your direction...
Because I know you're gonna need me to be strong...
Yes, they will have to come down harder with that hammer...
to even hope of silencing my song...

3 by 5 Card III

Back to the card that will keep me in check…
Three by five limit. I say, "What the heck !"

Why write forever…hey, why write at all ?
Out goes a story and In comes a call…

First comes the planning - second, the change…
Schedule your life…and then, rearrange…

Why write a volume when 'shortness' is king…
Brevity…Levity - that's what I sing…

Too much time wasted with whimsy and wit…
3 by 5 card, you know when to quit...

To Live or to Write (must there be a choice ?)

The ideal way is to write while you're doing...
To chart the pursuit as you do the pursuing...
The freshest of feelings will flower your verses...
So, ready your pen for the kisses and curses...

And carry your paper to parties and places...
And chronicle life as you find it in faces
of people you meet in the high - and the by - ways...
(It's not very neat, but it's now one of my ways...)

To be or to write is no longer the riddle...
For, whether you ponder or whether you piddle,
it's living that matters - today is the time !
So, look as you live it - and run as you rhyme...

I'm hoping you see what I've managed to utter...
and pardon the stains on this page, It's just butter.
This mess - it was caused by concurrently cooking
along with my rhyming...and eating...and looking...

OVERLOADED

Words upon words upon words upon pages...
(Maybe I'm just in the last of my 'stages')

Crowded and cluttered and crammed full of phrases...
Here in my mind I climb mountains of mazes...

Reading and looking at books full of notions...
Drowning in letters and paragraph-oceans...

Maybe I just need just a day at the park...
Maybe - a walk...or a time in the dark...
Maybe - a rigorous rub on my back...
Maybe - a tumble with sex-in-the-sack...

Maybe...just maybe...my one greatest need:
A Natural Law that forbids me to read...

EMMA WOOD CAMPGROUNDS......1990

I didn't want lines on this uncharted page...
I brought the wrong tablet, and now, in a rage,
I ponder events that escape my control,
and deep in a part of a piece of my soul,
the rusty chains rattle...the dust starts to stir...
and dreams of the battle begin to unblur...
My limbs slowly turn to the heat and the light...
My brain starts to burn and my heart says, "All right !"

I'm back on my feet and I'm taking a stand -
"To hell with this Paper ! I'm back in command !"

I'll write how I want to - above - or below...
or crossways...or sideways...or sloppy...or slow...

It's great ! What a feeling ! What freedom ! What fun !
The lines disappear as you fly...as you run...

And, once again, life plays a trick on this boy -
His rhyme-loving wife has a pome to enjoy...

MESSAGE TO MONICA

Monica isn't writing…
Nothing around to read…
Doesn't she know that her pomes and her dreams
are the 'uppers' that all of us need ?

Doesn't she see it's a little more sad when she
hides all her rhythms and rhymes ?
No other person is filling her spaces,
or taking her places and times…

Monica hasn't been writing…
Nothing to read but a book…
All of us searching thru dusty old pages…
Ev'ryone needs a 'new look'…

Ev'ryone else used to stop and remember the
'stars' that would 'shine' in her verse…
Somebody, please - get her writing again -
before it gets any worse...

I will write about it all

It comes to mind to write of things…
Whatever now the moment brings…
The whiskey and the wit command…
With hope in heart…with pen in hand…

With no restrictions…no restraint…
To write what 'IS'…and not what 'AIN'T'…
To let the feelings freely flow…
and go where they're compelled to go…

The people and the places call…
and I must write about it all…

THE CLIFF HOUSE

Most of my writing and all of my raging are
Done in the trenches where battles are waging...I

Make all these plans for a little vacation, but
When I arrive there is no inspiration...I

Sit by the seashore and stare at the ocean...my
Mind tries to think but it's lulled by the motion...the

Peace of the ebbing, the calm of the flowing ...(I
Should know, by now, where I go when I'm going)...the

Beach is ideal for respite and rest, but the
Waves aren't conducive to writing-your-best, so it's

Back to the war-zone of Mondays and work...(Is it
Natural law or a personal quirk ?)...but the

Struggles of people with Life's rights and wrongs are the
Stuff of my stories, the words of my songs...and, My

Friend, let me tell you: the joke's still on me...for I
Just wrote this pome by the edge of the sea...

FUCKIN' WORDS

I know that FUCK's a dirty word...it
Shouldn't be said and shouldn't be heard...but
Really, now, it's just a word...and
In a sense, it's so absurd...that

FUCK should cause such great alarm...you
Know, it doesn't do much harm...and
Nowadays it's used a lot...it's
One of the strongest words we got...when

I say 'FUCK', my kids stop 'dead'...my
Wife looks up - her face turns red...and
They can tell how deep I feel...when
I say 'FUCK', it's a big big deal...I

Don't say 'FUCK' for something small...some
Days I don't say 'FUCK' at all...and
Ev'ry fourth or second week...well,
'Heck's' the coarsest thing I speak...you

See, a word is just a sound...and
What it means gets kicked around...and
Talk is cheap (I've always stressed)...so
All our speech is poor - at best...it's

What we 'do' that's gonna last...when
All the fucking words are past...it's
'Who-loved-who' and 'who-was-kind'...and
Who brought back the lost and blind...and

FUCK, it ain't the sermons preached...it's
Who was touched and Who was reached...and
Who got up each time they fell...and
Who helped who - not who said 'hell'...well

Heck, I guess I made my point...I
Hope you're not bent out of joint.......I'm
Not as hard as it appears...Hey,
Diff'rent words hurt diff'rent ears...and

Shucks, if I've offended you, I've
Really not intended to...but
SHIT ! I get so fuckin' pissed, when
People put me on their list for
What I say, not what I do...(Is
That the way you're treated too ?)...you

Know, I guess it could be worse...I
Could be lying in my hearse...and
Some would pray and some would curse, "Thank God
For no more fucking verse !"

A Promise is a Promise

Here I am sitting and trying to write...
Sometimes it's easy - sometimes - uptight...
Sometimes I find I have nothing to say...
(Promised myself I would write ev'ry day...)

Pen on the paper - my mind in a vault...
Nothing is happ'ning - it isn't my fault...
Pen on the paper - I'm ready to start...
No one can say I'm not doing my part...

What can you do when your brain is a blank ?...
Pick out a word - and give it a crank...
O.K., I'll try it - what's there to lose...
Page thru a book - and randomly choose...

O.K., I've done it and 'AND' is the one...
(Give me a break ! This ain't any fun...)
'AND'...oh, forget it - this is absurd...
What can you do with that kind of word ?

How can I work with this kind of stuff ?
(I kept my promise - enough is enough.)

I GOT TO THINKIN'

(this is what happens when you want to write but have absolutely no inspiration......)

i got to thinkin'

of cabbages and kings

of a multiplicity of things

of the sparrow who sings

of eternal springs

of a lover who clings

of the last bell that rings

of a pong that pings

of a dent that dings

of a tinker that tings.......a shrinker that shrings..............a blinker that blings................

Scribbles on a napkin

Scribbles on a napkin...
Thoughts that come and go...
Maybe two will stay a while...
Maybe one will grow...

Why so many reasons
make so little sense...
Why there's so much int'rest in the
price of recompense...

Why so few beginnings
never find an end...
Why we search for wisdom in
the laughter of a friend...

When I Write Pomes

When I write pomes - I don't give a damn...
I throw around words with a crash ! bang ! bam !

Deficient in meter - reluctant to rhyme,
They never make sense one/third of the time...

What can you do when you do what you can ?...
I used to write straight - like a button-down man...

Used to use grammar invented in schools...
Made ev'ry rhythm conform to their rules...

Poetry properly cornered and squared...
Nobody read it and nobody cared...

One summer day - call it blind luck...
One of my thoughts started running amok...

My pencil was seized with a sort of a force, and
I wrote, "Holy Shit ! We are heading off course !"

Ever since then - life's been a breeze...
My pomes are allowed to go where they please...

They're still never read - but now I don't care...
(Hey, whoever said that writing was fair ?)

BASKET TWO:
Poh-Por-Ree

THE THINGS THAT ABIDE...

I look at the things and the deeds that I do...
And the time rushes in way before I get through...

And it rushes...pursues me and pushes me on...
And nothing is finished before it is gone...

So, I partly do that and I partly do this...
And my past is becoming a junkyard abyss,

filling up fast with unfinished starts...
where half-hearted horses pull unchartered carts...

And unspoken speeches get stuck in my throat...
I'm a captainless crew in a rudderless boat...

And they tell me I'm only a child of the Age...
And the world is too busy to notice my rage...

But, I'd just like to mention before I check out...
(in case there's a chance of a trace of a doubt...)

I WILL NOT BE PUSHED BY THE TIME OR THE TIDE...
AND I WILL NOT TREAT LIGHTLY THE THINGS THAT
ABIDE...

NOW I WISH YOU GOOD MORNING
(A song I wrote long long ago)

Now I wish you good morning on this morning of your life...
And my wishes will go with you on your way...
I cannot tell you what is hidden in the mountains you will climb...
But everything will come to you in time...
In time, the laughter...
In time, the pain...
What you will lose...
What you must gain...
What you will learn...
What you will teach...
Everything is there within your reach...
Reach out ! Reach out!

You'll find them hidden in the mountains you will climb...
The many wonders of the simple and sublime...
And some will come to you in reason...
Some will come to you in rhyme...
But everything shall come to you in time...

Some vows will break...
Some dreams will die...
Some plans you make you'll find are castles in the sky...
But through it all, if you find love...
You will reach the mountain top above...
With love ! With love !

And when tomorrow's just a dream of yesterday...
You may remember what an old fool had to say...
"In all the lessons of a lifetime only one I'm certain of...
Everything shall come to you in love"

Yes, everything shall come to those who love...
Yes, everything shall come to you in love...

A Kind of Compromise

The papers pile higher...and the reasons
don't make sense...
And the dying of desire is my only
recompence...

I can turn and look around me...down these
bureaucratic aisles...
And imagine all the madness that is
filling up the files...

I can turn again and wonder if the
worth of what I do...
will be measured by the Measurer
who measures what is true...

I can only hope that someday where
those meetings never end...
They will not decide my future
while they're playing 'let's pretend'...

And the paperwork keeps piling and
the Lost have lost control...
I can't silence any longer all the
stirrings in my soul...

For, the answers have no meanings...
And the problems never change...
And I keep on filling folders up with
words I rearrange...

And the papers pile higher...Hey, I
know it cannot last...
So I try to find my patience in
the lessons of the past...

And I settle for the solace in the
knowing I was right...
When they said the sun was shining
in the middle of the night...

LITTLE CHILD (lyrics to a song)

Little Child, you come to me with teardrops...
Broken toy and broken heart to mend...
Dry your tiny eyes, for I will mend them...
At least I'll try...
Now don't you cry...

We can build a newer toy tomorrow...
And we can dream a better dream tonight...
So put away the pieces and the sorrow...
Just for tonight -
It'll be alright...Little Child...

For I recall another child from long long ago...
With a broken toy and nowhere he could go...
And I can still remember him crying in the night...
And no one in the night
to hold him tight...

So, Little Child, I will not leave you lonely...
Together we will see this to the end...
And you will find that broken toys and even broken hearts
Somehow always mend...
They always work again...
And you'll be smiling then...Little Child...

For, all I know is: Love's the only healer...
And all I've learned is: Love can stop the pain...
And when I go, it will not matter, Little Child...
I'll stay just long enough...
And you'll be strong enough...
To love again...

And you will know that Love's the only healer…
And you will learn that Love can stop the pain…
And when I go, it will not matter, Little Child…
I'll stay just long enough…
And you'll be strong enough…
To love again...

THE BIG PICTURE

You know it isn't easy, with the troubles comin' down,
To keep the 'bigger picture' in our view...
You know it isn't easy to recall the total plan -
With four weeks mortgage payments overdue...

Oh, sure, the Master's Blueprint has a place for each of us...
We're travelers in space - and flyin' blind...
But when your ass is runnin' thru that alligator swamp,
It's hard to keep the 'picture' in your mind...

We keep our asses runnin' from the madness that we fear...
And try to keep our eyes upon the stars...
But it ain't easy reachin' for that rainbow in the sky
When all our dreams get covered up with scars...

Now, me - I'm just another sort of runner with the pack...
And you - well, I can tell you've done your share...
And I'm so very grateful that we're runnin' side by side -
It won't last long - but who are we to care...

For we have shared our visions of the 'Picture' and we know...
And we have had our laugh...or two...or three...
And we have led the madness on a very merry chase...
And had ourselves believing we'd be free...

So, thanks again for bringing by your special kind of smile...
And thanks again for telling me your tale...
You know it isn't easy "keepin' on" and "lookin' up"
But - I'll remember you - and I WON'T FAIL...

One for the Road

The road that led us far away
has led us back again…
It doesn't give us answers…
It won't tell us where or when…

It beckons and we follow it…
and one day long ago,
Our lives - they ran together…
But just why ? We'll never know…

But why ? We'll never really care…
Because we had the best -
Part of it was friendship
that always stood the test…

Part of was laughter
and learning how to give…
and part of it was growing
and finding how to live…

And part of it was stronger
than anything we know -
the 'part' that's still within us…
No matter where we go…

The part that says, "Lead on, You Road,
"Who cares how far apart…
"It travels with us where we go - the love
that's in our heart."

So, here's a toast to Travelers…
May, ev'ry now and then,
the road be kind - for 'auld lang syne' -
and lead us back again...

MEETINGS (X@$%!?&!?)

Monday morning meeting...
People sit around...
Listen to the leaders...
Sentences of sound...

State the main objectives...
Principles and goals...
Words devoid of meaning...
Logic full of holes...

Expectations listed...
"Let me hear your view."
Nothing ever happens...
Nothing's ever new...

Total wasted moments...
(No, that isn't fair.)
There's a greater reason
keeps me in my chair...

There's a plan I follow...
Charts I've learned to trust...
and the course I've chosen
is the course I must....

Where it leads is hazy...
(I no longer ask.)
All I know: IT MATTERS
Just to do the task...

So, I sit in meetings...
Write reports in rhyme...
Someone will explain it all...
in His own good time...

GOLD STRIKE

I was poor till yesterday…
When I struck gold…
A vein as wide as main street…
Riches manifold…

For as I walked down main street…
I heard a blind man sing…
And suddenly I realized…
This was a golden thing…

Then, as I turned the corner…
A beggar smiled at me…
And in his simple joy I found…
The wealth of poverty…

And just as I began to wonder…
Where it all would end…
Somewhere further down the road…
A stranger called me 'friend'…

Thus ran my luck on main street…
Why ? I cannot say…
A simple stroll down main street…
And I am rich today…

HARD TIMES

'HARD TIMES' is a good good teacher...
Say what you will, but I know what I say...
Better that poet, professor, or preacher...his
Lessons remain till your last living day...

'HARD TIMES' is a wise old companion...
Harder than hell when he's gotta be tough...
Crawl to the summit or drop to the canyon...
No greater school than the road that is rough...

Millions of lectures that stutter and stammer...
Thousands of textbooks to show you the way...
Gimme a hit on the head with a hammer...
and I won't forget what you wanted to say...

A Wish, a Prayer, a Toast - to the Middle Manager

I cling to my log in the swells of the water...
See, I'm a survivor of storms and of slaughter...

At first I would struggle with swimming and sinking...
With wasted emotions and unthoughtful thinking...

I struggled with sharks. I got bitter and battered...
I cared about things that just shouldn't have mattered...

The flotsam of memos so hurriedly written...
The unending crises - I thought about quitting...

The non-stopping changes that deluge my in-box...
(Hey, some of my peers now reside in a tin box...)

But I'm a survivor and nothing can drown me...
I flow with the ebbs and the tides that surround me...

And, once in a while, when it's calm in the ocean...
Away in the distance, a sound and a motion...

And, what is that speck that the waves are ping-ponging?
Another poor soul with a log and a longing...

A shout from the deep, "Is that you still afloat there?"
"You bet!", I yell back. "You've a helluva boat there."

Well, here's to the legions of lonely survivors...
The old weathered captains...the new green arrivers...

Let's send them a prayer as a beacon to guide them...
Or drink them a toast...or at least, not deride them...

And wish them smooth sailing through helter and skelter...
And final safe passage to shoreline and shelter...

SOME NAMES AREN'T AS SIMPLE AS GEORGE BERNARD SHAW'S

Listen, my children, and please give a pause.
If you're in need of a care or a cause.
Take up the banner of Bonnie J. Tawse.

She's been a victim of life's little flaws.
People address her with 'hems' and with 'haws'.
Somehow her name seems to stick in their craws.

Sure, you may say that they've broken no laws.
She, nonetheless, has been grasping at straws,
trying to search for a clue or a clause.

Why don't they just get in touch with their jaws ?
Nobody's tongue trips on words spelt like 'gauze'.
Nobody's troubled by last names like 'Claus'.
What's so damn terribly tough about 'Tawse' ??

(Frankly, we owe her a round of applause.)

Ah Yes, I remember it well

Who should I thank
for yesterday…
For a lovely girl
Who chanced my way ?

For a sunny sky
and a summer breeze…
And a sun-warmed lake
and a million trees…

Each hill was a fountain
flowing free…
Flooding the fields
with greenery…

Each cloud was a care
drifting away…
And to top it all,
the month was May…

Who should I thank
for a sky of blue…
And the joy of sharing it
all with you…

What really made it
a perfect day…
The lovely girl…
or the month of May ?

DON'T ANALYZE ME'S

Please...please...
Please...please...
Don't try to try
to analyze me's...

Don't try to guess
Why I do what I do...
What I mean when I say,
"It's a quarter past two."

Don't go explaining
the nonsense you see...
If I'm eating a book –
Just let it be...

For, most of the time
I am what I am...
I dare what I dream
and I don't give a damn...

And when I'm in water,
it's cuz I'm too hot...
or maybe I'm thirsty...
or maybe I'm not...

And if I say, "Hi !",
I want you to know
I simply am really am
saying, "Hello !"

So, don't look for reasons
when things are askew...
You'll be better off
when I say "I love you."

THE HAMMERS OF LIFE

And when tomorrow comes around with all its thunder...
And I awake to face the hammer comin' down...
I'll be O.K., my friend, so don't you wonder...
For one more time I'll pick myself up off the ground...

And I will take another step in your direction...
Because I know you're gonna need me to be strong...
Yes, they will have to come down harder with that hammer...
Because they're never ever gonna stop my song...

'Long time coming' (lyrics to a song)

It's been a long time coming and a short way to go...
And the race is running, I know...
And there are no reasons for the deeds that must be done...
It's been a long hot season in the sun...

It's been a hard hard journey with no one by my side...
And the hills are climbing...and so
We must walk together...or we stand alone...
It's been a hard hard long-time journey home...

And I long to see my homeland
And I'm tired of being no-man...
I'm a slow-talkin' fast-drivin' doughman...
GET ME BACK ! TAKE ME BACK! TAKE ME BACK !

I have carried the crosses of the mighty and the meek...
I have borne the burdens of the wicked and the weak...
I have wept for the soldier, I have prayed for the slave...
I will march on forever till my feet are in my grave...

I will march on forever till my feet are in my grave...
There is someone who needs me - there is someone I must save
If you search for me forever you will find me forever
If you need me forever I will need you forever
Put your hand in mine forever I will hold your hand forever
If you love me forever I will love you forever
If you love me forever I will love you forever
If you love me forever I will love you forever

I will love you forever till my feet are in my grave...

POLI-SCI CLASS

(Many many years ago I was sitting in this very very boring
political-science class. I felt trapped. I couldn't stand it any
longer. Hence, this ode to freedom.)

Poli-sci class !
What a gas !
Sometimes I feel I've sat in here
And dreamed away another year –
A year that would have, probably,
Meant more to me, had I been free
To do the things I'd rather do
(To do what I've been meaning to)
Like take some walks I've put aside
Like try some tricks I haven't tried
Like sing some songs I've only hummed
Like read some books thru which I've thumbed
Like simply sitting 'neath a tree
and wondrin' why some men are free
to follow any star that nods,
to take their chance with any odds.
While, on the other hand, I find
some men with bars across their mind,
who won't take time to turn their head
and watch the stars fall overhead,
who close their eyes and say they see,
who lock their hearts and say they're free.

Sometimes I'd rather lose a year
than spend it wondrin' why I'm here.
I'm here, and what is more, I'm free.
Why analyze a liberty ?

TWAS A LONG TIME COMING

Twas a long time coming...
Twas a short way here...
Twas a desert learning...
Twas an ocean prayer...

Twas a lover's leavings...
So, we couldn't stay...
Couldn't take the grievings...
Twas the only way...

Now and now I wonder...
Will the journey end ?
Rend it all asunder...
Build it up again...

Twas a touch by nightfall...
Twas a hope by dawn...
Yes, it was the right call...
To keep keepin' on...

Did just what we had to...
Never thought it out...
Did just what we had to...
Never had a doubt...

Twas a long time coming...
Twill be over soon...
Come......catch us running...
Up...across the moon...

THIS VERSE IS NOT FREE...BUT THE ADVICE IS (1997)

Me ? Give advice ?

No, not much anymore...

Maybe a nod, one direction or other...

Maybe an 'either' or 'or'...

Maybe a smaller suggestion or two, in the evening and over a drink...

Maybe a nudge, but that's it and it's over. Time for a party, I think...

People will only believe what you do. They seldom believe what you say.

Don't waste much time on the telling and teaching. Do it ! Live it ! Today !

Actions will say it much louder than words...well,

Excuse me, my pen's blown a fuse...

Here comes a loser who needs some assistance...

Gotta go walk in his shoes...

DON'T WEEP FOR ME (a song)

Well I am just a lonely travellin' man…
I go along and do the best I can…
The road that I must travel is the road of misery…
And you could never weep enough for me…

Each day I see the soldiers marching by…
Young men who must fight and don't know why…
But I will find the answer though it takes eternity…
And you could never weep enough for me…

You could cry an ocean full of sorrow and regret
And never pay the price for what they gave…
You could cry a hundred years - the world would not forget
The questions that still echo from the grave…

And so I guess that I'll be on my way…
To sing another song another day…
Save your tears for young men and the love they'll never
see…
For you could never weep enough for me…

HOLLYWOOD

They call my town the tinsel town
Where 'make believe' is king
Where ev'rybody wears a mask
Where glamour is 'the thing'

They say my town is built on dreams
Well, maybe this is true
Perhaps we tend to 'play the role'
More than others do

And yet, my friends, consider this,
That when we play our parts
We work a kind of miracle
Within a million hearts

And when we laugh upon the screen
A million faces smile
And when we cry, the world forgets
Its troubles for a while

So, friends, be kind to 'tinsel town'
For, strange as it may seem,
It hates to share the spotlight
But...it loves to share its dream

November 2, 1987...on the way to work

...early mornin' comin' down...
Not a lot of noise around...
...breakfast in a quiet place...
Summerland...and now I face

One more day and one more chance...
Will it drag ? or will it dance ?

I have hunches in my mind...
Clues of what I just might find...
(You can bet there'll be some hurt.)
Got to keep my soul alert.
Got to put my smile on tight.
(Keep my sorrows out of sight.)

Someone's gonna need my care.
Someone's got to find me there.
Life is hard...but, yes, it's fair...
Just get ready...just prepare.
I might be the second chance
For one who didn't get to dance.......

SIMPLE THINGS (a song)

Seems this sad old world is movin' on much too fast...
The simple things we love do not last...
Wise men try to show you why your dreams have gone astray...
And ev'ry wise man points a diff'rent way....

And all the laughter of the morning of our lives
Is just an echo in the songs we try to sing...
But in the darkness of the evening there's a few hearts still believing
That the answer is a plain and simple thing...

Come be my friend
Drink my wine
Break my bread
Take my time...
We won't let simple things be forgotten...

You see them on the city streets and freeways...
People drivin' hard and goin' nowhere...
Cattle runnin' blind to rivers they won't find
And heaven help the few that really mind...

Can't we remember all the yearnings of our youth ?
Have we forgotten how we hungered for the truth ?
I don't know what's happening to hearts that once were free...
I only know just what it's done to me...

I need a friend to drink my wine
Break my bread
And take my time
We won't let simple things be forgotten...
Yes, the simple things must never be forgotten...
Oh, the simple things will never be forgotten...

ANTS

My thoughts keep going back to when
My age was nine – or maybe ten…
And we were poor (or so I'm told…
I didn't know – at ten years old…)

And – anyway – at ten or nine
I got along just very fine…
And ev'ry day, when school was through –
I knew exactly what to do…

I'd run right home and grab a snack,
Put on my shorts and head out back…
And ev'ry day I'd find 'em there –
A million of 'em – everywhere !!!

The big red ants who bit and stung –
And I was gonna kill each one…
My fav'rite weapons, I recall:
A hammer and a tennis ball…

The tennis ball was really neat –
You'd bounce it on them in the street…
And, if you bounced it straight and fast –
Well…none of them would make it past…

But, sometimes I would miss and then –
One ant would live – to bite again…
The hammer wasn't quite as fun –
But it would never miss a one…

It killed them sure and killed them dead,
But, left a banging in my head…
(And after one and forty years,
I still have ringing in my ears…)

Well, anyway – you learn and grow,
And there is one thing that I know:
For killing ants – both large and small,
It's best to use a tennis ball...

I also learned another thing –
It's hard to hear above a ring...
(And maybe, on a diff'rent score,
The ants have really won the war...)

Back on the Monday

Back on the 'Monday'...and settle-ing in...
Kind of a dream: what I've done...where I've been...

Feelin' the force of the time and the day...
Work to be done...well, what can I say...

What's there to do but to stretch out my limbs...
This ain't the place for the prayers and the hymns...

This is the moment of gettin' it done...
Doin' my part in the makin' it run...

Taking my job and putting it first...
The most and the least - the best and the worst...

All of the stuff in the life of a day....
Back in the jungle...well, what can I say...

November 7, 1965...at the Ashbaugh's

There's a lot to be said for a night like tonight...
Where the day and its worries are hidden from sight...
The dark and the quiet remind us of peace...
We forget, for a moment, that wars never cease...

There's a lot to be said for a home that will share
All its song and its laughter - and not give a care
Whose pockets are rich, or whose sayings are smart...
As it opens its door, so it opens its heart...

There's a lot to be said for friends such as these...
You can say what you like - you can do as you please...
Welcome you'll be, whether wise man or fool...
Just be who you are is the one simple rule...

There's a lot to be said for the nectar we taste...
But the greatest of praise is to not let it waste...
So, let's drink and be gay till our glasses run dry...
The blessings we have - too soon pass us by...

Deep in the City

Deep in the city...no sunshine...no flowers...
Dreams are as cheap as a bottle of wine...
Bodies are bought for a couple of hours...
Boys without shoes try to sell you a shine...

Deep in the city, below the clean towers,
Newspaper Joe had a stand on the street...
Selling his papers at regular hours...
Always a smile on his face when we'd meet...

All of us people - in suits - in a hurry...
Came for the 'NEWS" from this ragged-clothed man...
'HEADLINES' and columns to add to our worry...
Buy 'em up - read 'em as fast as we can...

Deep in the city, well, something was funny...
'We' ran in circles while 'he' took it slow...
One day I asked him as he took my money,
"Tell me your secret, cuz I've got to know."

Newspaper Joe, he just smiled and moved slowly...
took me aside as he lowered his head...
Then in a voice that was heavy and holy -
"Life is an elbow." was all that he said.

SEVEN DREAMS

Seven dreams I had one night...
And I remember, but not quite...

ONE was hope, forever stilled...
TWO was desire, unfulfilled...
THREE was ev'ry wish I made,
...when time was young and life was played...
FOUR was just a wise old man.
...learning foolishness again...
FIVE was a plan the world had tried...
...but somehow all the blueprints lied...
SIX was a minute, more or less
...of eternal happiness...
SEVEN was a hungry throng
who cried, "Wake up ! And start a song !"

TAKE A BREAK (c. 1970)

Just a note to catch your eye...
Just to tell you, by and by...
When the work is piling high...
Take a little break...

Just a note from someone who
Always thinks a lot of you...
Always worries what you do -
Do it for my sake...

Just a word to trip your mind...
Make you stop - and go unwind...
(Paperwork can make you blind.)
Good advice to take...

Take the time to smell a flower...
Just a minute - not an hour...
Keep your soul from going sour...
Give yourself a break !

AROUND THE BEND

Don't send me letters from way down the river...
They're full of worries that never come true...
Sailing today is all I can handle...
Keeping the course is all I can do...

(Chorus)

All in good time, my friend, my friend...
All in good time, my friend...
Coming in reasons and coming in rhyme...
All in the good good time...

Used to read tea leaves and palms for a penny...
Needed to know what tomorrow would bring...
Would it be little ? Would it be many ?
Would it be beggar ? Would it be king ?

Will there be sorrow for Jennie and Johnny ?
Will there be sunshine for Maggie and Mel ?
Only two choices in all of our choosing...
Living or dying - heaven or hell...

Now I'm contented with daydreams and drifting...
Couldn't care less how it's all gonna end...
All in good time - the fog will be lifting...
All in good time - the rounding the bend...

All in good time, my friend, my friend...
All in good time, my friend...
Coming in reasons and coming in rhyme...
All in the good good time...

Cost of a Traffic Light

Mister Politician,
What's the price today ?
Just how much, exactly,
will we have to pay ?

Life so young, so full of promise -
Now forever stilled…
Hope so bright, so full of yearning -
Dead and unfulfilled…

Laughter of a girl who'll never
see another spring…
Beauty of soul who had
so little time to sing…

All the joy she might have known…
The dreams she might have dared…
All the truth she might have learned…
The love she might have shared…

Mister Politician,
What's the price today ?
Just how much, exactly,
will we have to pay ?

TOMORROW

I'm not too sure of those days to come…
Will the time crawl ? Will the time run ?
Will I complete anything I've begun ?
I only know Tomorrow…

I have no goals for the future days…
No chartered course for my wand'ring ways…
I try to set goals - but nothing stays…
I only see Tomorrow…

Tomorrow's short and close at hand…
A simple task for a simple man…
Yes, I can handle a one-day plan…
I only want Tomorrow…

SIX LESSONS

Six sort-of lessons
I'm sending to you…
Seven's too many -
Five are too few…

Six kind-of crutches
that helped me along…
(I don't know to whom
they origin'ly belonged…)

But six is enuf…
and the First is quite plain:
Love is the healer
that stops all the pain…

Talking is cheap…
(my favorite quote…)
and so is - almost -
ev'ry line that I wrote…

Lesson, the Third,
is easy to reach:
"You want to unwind ?
Go walk on the beach…"

Pray for your mother,
no matter what's past…
This is the Fourth
and nearly the last…

"Whatever you do,
Make it care, make it count…"
I'm stopping at Five,
it's a better amount...

One of Yesterday's Boys

Tomorrow, tomorrow is yesterday
We'll soon outrun the sun...
The deeds we plan to do next year
Already have been done...

The schemes we plan to test in time
are old and overdue...
Barely we begin to wish
and we must wish anew...

Time and the age fill us with lies...
Today is a decade ago...
The clock is ticking out memories...
and few there are who know...

And few there are who feel the force
and fury with which we fly...
Shaken, our spirits - hurried, our hearts...
and if we delay, we die...

    Oh, how I long for a slow growing tree
    and the calm of a slow winding stream...
    An hour that's sixty full minutes long...
    One hour to sit and dream...

    Oh, how I yearn for an out-dated soul
    who has more than a second to spare...
    A friend who has learned that a broken bond
    is the hardest cross to bear...

Gathering blessings as few as these
I'd surrender Tomorrow's brief joys...
Gladly I'd leave this time and this age
And become one of Yesterday's boys...

BUREAUCRAT

The work I do is madness -
Labor without sense -
It seems a hundred years without a fire...

The paperwork...the memos -
Reports about reports -
Systems without passions and desire...

The work I do is madness -
I do it real well -
Its logic's locked within me like a vise...

I take their crazy reasons
and I make them sound quite clear -
Lies can sound so true when they're precise...

But I grow tired of madness -
and now it isn't fun -
The doing doesn't do it any more...

And I must taste again
of things that really count -
or very shortly I will be no more...

Hey, I'm sick of playing games -
That's all that's left, the playing -
(Though, in my time, I've won at quite a few.)

But if it doesn't happen soon,
it will not happen late -
and I'll become the madness that I do...

AN INTERRUPTED MAN

Today is just another in a series of todays...
And days - they never go as you would like...
It seems you do your planning and you measure all the
ways...
And - suddenly - the schedule 'goes on strike'...

At nine a.m. you plan to sit and write a long report...
At nine-o-five the phone begins to ring...
At nine-o-five-and-change your brain is signaling, "ABORT"
And you start doing quite a diff'rent thing...

And here I am just wond'rin' where the road is gonna go...
I'd like to think that I am in control
By now I should know better, but I know it isn't so...
A million things keep tuggin' at my soul...

Perhaps I'll waste the hours in a deep and dirty book...
That's not what I intend - but who can tell ? ?
I've heard that, sometimes, people in a monastery nook
have ended up outside the gates of hell...

And even Paul, the preacher and apostle, used to do
the things he said, for sure, he never would...
And so - I guess - it's anybody's guess that me and you
will do or don't the deeds we could and should...

Today I take a walk around the building 'cross the street...
The air is cool and fresh and free...and, "Ahhh"...

The walking feels so good along the muscles in my feet...
And now - the day's a little more less-blah...

Which also makes me want to grab a pencil or a phone
To write someone or shout it thru the line:
"Hey, You - it's Me ! - it's true ! - you never walk alone...
"I called to let you know it feels 'so fine'...

"I called (or wrote) to tell you that the 'walking' gets you high
"And I would like you up here next to me...
"I bet you didn't plan to take a walk or see the sky...
"I bet you didn't plan to feel so free...

"I bet you never thought you'd get a letter or a call...
"And I had no intent to phone or write...
"But here we are together in the middle of it all...
"And evidently, there's no end in sight...

"Goodbye - and please remember, as you reconstruct your
plan...
"That life is more a prairie than a park...
"Consider this the counsel of an interrupted man...
"Who walks and waits and wonders in the dark."........

PEACEFUL SUNDAY MORN' (4/27/99)

Sunday mornin'...quiet now...
try to write some lines somehow...
...peaceful moment...cooling breeze...
Life of struggle – Life of ease...

This has been the life of mine...
never in the center line...
always up or always down..
always circlin' round and roun'...

Never really had a goal...
met a girl who saved my soul...
never really thought it out...
had a dream and had a doubt...
made decisions as they came...
never dodged the praise or blame...

Sunday mornin'...now the sun...
soon the day will start to run...
soon...the things I need to do...
fix the faucet...errands, too...

Phone calls comin'...answers sought...
Busy! Busy! Who'd of thought...
who'd of guessed at what life brings...
Children. Changes. Other things.

Who'd of seen how strange the ways...
Who'd of known how fast the days...

Sunday mornin'...reverie...
sunlight...silence...coffee...me...

About The Author

Bill Jennings is an 88 year old lover of life. He has five children by his first wife Merry, who died of leukemia. He lives in Portland, Oregon, with his second wife, Dora. He hopes his rhymes about writing, meetings and memos, and life put a smile in your day.

Made in the USA
Columbia, SC
12 August 2022

65199865R00039